THE SPIRIT OF
BRIGHTON & HOVE

Iain McGowan

HALSGROVE

First published in Great Britain in 2008

British Library Cataloguing-in-Publication Data
A CIP record for this title is available from the British Library

ISBN 978 1 84114 834 2

HALSGROVE
Halsgrove House
Ryelands Industrial Estate
Bagley Road, Wellington
Somerset TA21 9PZ
Tel: 01823 653777
Fax: 01823 216796
email: sales@halsgrove.com
website: www.halsgrove.com

Printed and bound by D'Auria Industrie Grafiche, Italy

Introduction

Exciting, exhilarating, elegant, trendy, diverse – the very word 'Brighton' has that mysterious ability to conjure up so many different images to so many minds. For some its attractions may be indefinable yet to others they are as clear-cut as the salty air on a winter's afternoon. It may simply be the sunshine or the quality of light, but perhaps above all, it is the city's spectacular contrasts. Graceful architecture sits with the extravagance of The Royal Pavilion; cockles and jellied eels on the 'prom' with oysters in The Lanes; day trippers with political party activists; antique shops with candy floss; long nights clubbing with bracing seafront rides on the Volks electric railway. This mix of culture and colour is probably Brighton's greatest fascination. The very words Brighton Rock are engraved in the English language, a magnet for those heading south from Victoria seeking the sea, striped deck chairs and fish and chips.

A colourful scene on the lower promenade. Originally this area was part of the beach below the old town. In the background is The Old Ship Hotel, the oldest inn in Brighton with records dating back to 1559.

Looking down on to the lower promenade from King's Road. Brighton Pier is in the distance.

The Lanes.

The numerous antique and jewellery shops, fashion outlets, pubs, cafés and restaurants to be found here make The Lanes one of the most picturesque areas of Brighton. In high summer the squares and pavements are filled with umbrella shaded tables and chairs, popular with residents and visitors alike. Shoppers saunter along narrow alleyways and artists and buskers abound.

9

By the late 1790s Brighton, as it was becoming known, was beginning to expand at a considerable rate into its new role as a seaside resort. But as the fishing industry declined, the old part of the town became an increasingly poor district of small, cramped fishermens' and tradesmens' housing and businesses. It was not until the dawn of the twentieth century that its charm began to be appreciated. Slowly many of the old cottages were converted into small shops that give The Lanes their distinctive and colourful character.

Towards the end of the nineteenth century there were over 700 drinking houses either as hotels, pubs or beer houses in Brighton and Hove. Within The Lanes several of the pub names give a hint of their past history.

In 1787 George, Prince of Wales, commissioned Henry Holland, a well-known architect, to design and build a seaside residence for him. Constructed on the site of an existing farmhouse, it had bow windows, balconies, and a central domed rotunda supported by columns and was called the Marine Pavilion.

In 1811 the Prince was elevated to Prince Regent and his ambitions of a grand palace were soon to be realised. Between the years 1815 to 1822 the highly respected architect John Nash transformed the Marine Pavilion into the amazing oriental extravagance that we know today as The Royal Pavilion. With its pagoda roofs, minarets, colonnades and onion-shaped domes it is Brighton's best-known building and possibly one of the most recognisable in Britain.

The interior of The Royal Pavilion was designed jointly by Frederick Crace and Robert Jones. The exotic schemes, with their rich and sophisticated decoration combined with the superb quality of the furnishings and furniture, created an appropriately magnificent setting for the new king.
Above left: The Banqueting Room. *Above right:* The Music Room.

The exterior of the Royal Stables and Riding House (now The Dome Concert Hall and Corn Exchange). Designed for the Prince of Wales by William Porden in an Indian Style, the building was built in the north-west corner of the pavilion grounds and completed in 1808.

Opposite page: Epitome of Summer. Looking east towards the Marina from Brighton Pier.

Brighton Town Hall was built in 1830 to a design by Thomas Cooper due to the desire of the town commissioners that Brighton should have a hall in keeping with its fashionable image. This rather grand classical building, on the site of the old market place, was completed in the year that King George IV died. It is still in use today but many of the offices of Brighton and Hove City Council have been moved to other areas of the city.

Charles Street with its small bow-windowed town houses, built about 1790.

Royal Crescent, Marine Parade was built between 1798 and 1807 on the cliff east of Old Steine. This series of houses has been described by Pevsner as the 'earliest unified composition of Brighton' and 'the earliest demonstration of a sympathy with sea and beach'.

Following on from the Royal Crescent, more unified architectural works started to appear both east and west of the Old Steine. Bedford Square, started in 1810, was the first square outside the old town to be built, followed eight years later by Regency Square shown here. Sited immediately opposite the West Pier and with its characteristic bow windows and verandas, many of its buildings are now used as hotels and guesthouses.

The blackened, fire ravaged and distorted skeleton of the West Pier. Brighton's West Pier, sited immediately opposite Regency Square, was opened in 1866.

Opposite page: A late winter's afternoon over the pier.

Brighton Pier at dusk. The third of Brighton's piers was opened in 1899 and soon became known as the Palace Pier. Described as the 'grandest pier ever built', it was over 500m long and its buildings, including a theatre and concert hall were designed in an oriental style to reflect that of The Royal Pavilion.

Gourmet or artists' delight! Brighton rock and candy floss.

Looking eastwards along Hove Promenade to Brighton in wintry conditions.

Opposite page: A hot August afternoon on the lower promenade and beach. The shattered structure of the West Pier lies in the background.

Artists' quarter on the lower promenade.

Colour, colour everywhere.

Fishing boats drawn up on the shingle beach at Hove. The name Hove was possibly derived from the Danish word 'Howe' meaning ancient burial place although no mention of Hove as such is given in the *Domesday Book*.

The Brighton Sea Life Centre, originally known as The Aquarium, was completed and opened to the public in 1872. It was designed by Eugenius Birch who also designed the West Pier. The underground Aquarium was an instant success, being visited by many crowned heads of Europe and other distinguished visitors from overseas.

This page and opposite: A lazy summer's day by the sea.

Cars from the annual veteran London/Brighton car run arriving at the finishing point in Madeira Drive. The first 'emancipation' run was held on 14 November 1896 and was organised by the then Motor Car Club to celebrate the Locomotive and Highways Act of that year.

Enthusiasts admiring the line up of vintage motor cycles in Madeira Drive after the completion of the 2004 Pioneer Run. Organised by the Motor Cycle Club, the historic rally was first started in 1937.

Brighton Marina. Part of the marina village clustered around the inner harbour area below the cliffs. During its entire history, Brighton has never had a harbour, having relied on its piers to serve both packet boats and pleasure steamers and, of course, its beach to haul fishing boats on to. Harbour schemes had been discussed for centuries but to no avail until 1963 when a massive combined marine, residential and entertainment complex was proposed. After eight years of considerable controversy, planning difficulties and parliamentary procedure, construction of the Brighton Marina started on a site below the cliffs just east of Kemp Town.

Spring colour on Palmeira Lawns. This fine square, at the eastern end of Church Road, Hove, is beautifully enhanced by its floral clock and surrounding Victorian buildings. The flint church of St John the Baptist, seen to the left of the photograph, complements the scene.

The clock tower at the junction of Queen's Road with Western Road and North and West Streets is one of Brighton's best known landmarks. Built in 1888 and described by Pevsner as 'worthless' it is now a much-loved symbol of the town.

The interior of Brighton Station fronting on to Queen's Road. The first railway line to reach Brighton was that from Shoreham opening on 11 May 1840 and followed soon after by the main line from London opened on 21 September 1841.

Scenes of the Sunday Market near Brighton Station. Every Sunday morning a large Bric-a-Brac/Antiques Market is held on the site of the old locomotive works adjacent to the station.

From the raised site of the locomotive works this view is obtained looking across the rooftops of North Laine to the curving viaduct of the Brighton-Lewes railway line that dominates this area. Beyond are the terraces and streets above Preston Park.

The University of Sussex, Falmer. A university was first proposed for Brighton in 1911 when a fund for its establishment was started at a public meeting in The Royal Pavilion.

Racing at Brighton. Informal challenge races were run on Whitehawk Down (later known as Race Hill), as early as the beginning of the eighteenth century, but it was not until 1783 that the first official Brighton races were organised by a group of leading inhabitants. The course itself is about 2.5 km long and regarded as extremely fast, much of it being downhill. Some of the world's fastest racing times have been set over its length.

Jubilant Brighton and Hove Albion football supporters outside Kings House on Grand Avenue, Hove, celebrating their team's promotion to First Division football in the 2001-2002 season.

The Brighton Festival first started in 1967 under the artistic direction of Ian Hunter. Featuring a mix of world-class artists with more informal and local talent, the festival, despite some shaky periods, continues to provide highly popular entertainment during most of the month of May each year.

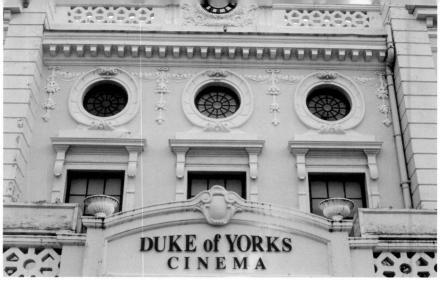

The Duke of York's Cinema at Preston Circus is one of the earliest purpose-built cinemas still operating in the country.

Opposite page: Throughout the year the city features a flourishing and exciting cultural life.

The colourful entrance panels to the old Hippodrome Theatre. Opened as a variety theatre in Middle Street in 1901 after a short period as an ice rink, the Hippodrome was one of the most popular theatres in Brighton. Closed in 1965 the Hippodrome is now a Bingo Hall although much of its original decoration, such as these panels and parts of the interior, remain intact.

Opposite page: The Theatre Royal in New Road.

The enclosed Churchill Square shopping centre off Western Road was built in the late 1990s at a cost of about £90 million. Re-developed from the earlier 1960s scheme, it is a vast improvement in both shopping and aesthetic terms.

Opposite page: The central atrium with lift and escalators to the three principal shopping levels.

The circular flint dovecot at Patcham Court Farm is the only scheduled ancient monument within the city. Built in the seventeenth century or earlier, with walls 1m thick and containing 550 nesting recesses, it still retains its original swinging ladder and roof access for the birds.

During the First World War, The Royal Pavilion was used as a hospital for wounded Indian soldiers, over 4000 men being nursed back to health. Muslims who died were buried at Woking, but Hindus and Sikhs were cremated on funeral pyres at this beautiful downland site behind Patcham and their ashes scattered in the sea. The Chattri Memorial was erected on the site of these cremations in their honour.

The Foredown Tower. Built in 1909 on the edge of the Downs behind Portslade, the Foredown Tower was constructed as a water tower to the Foredown Isolation Hospital, also known as the Hove Sanatorium.

Brighton and Hove were themselves just small communities at one time but as they grew and developed they encompassed many of the surrounding villages and hamlets. Sometimes there is little that remains of the original village apart from the church, yet in others traditional flint, timber boarded or cobble faced cottages give a hint of their community's past history.

Opposite page: The peaceful scene looking across the village pond at Falmer on a fine winter's morning.